Painting Landscapes From Imagination

Magunta Dayakar

Copyright reserved 2019
Magunta Venkata Subba Reddy (alias Magunta Dayakar)

Other Books on Art from Magunta Dayakar
How To Start A Painting And How to Plan It?
How To Finish A Painting?

Contents

Writer's Note 1
No words of introduction... 2
Imagination... 8
    Imagination ... What is it?... 9
    From Imagination 10
    How do you know 11
    I know it always happens 13
    Those Three 15
    Observation ... how it works?... 17
    Relations 19
    It's the same here.. 22
    Then how do you say 24
    Summary.. 27
The Power Of Imagination.. 28
    Why most of the artists are not successful in this 29
    Is this problem happening to all artists of all ages? 31
How it happens from imagination?... 33
Demo... 36
Painting from Imagination - Demo... 37
Imagination plays a key role.. 49
Final Painting... 53
Concluding Words 58
About Magunta Dayakar... 59

Writer's Note

As I said in my previous books, I am writing about one or two issues in every book. In this book as well, it is the same. I am writing about 'Painting from Imagination ' in this book. This book is for art students and artists.

When I tried to find books on how to develop imagination, I did not find any proper books to understand it in a simple way without breaking my head on complex theories. Imagination is a critical skill for artists. Since there were no books to meet our requirement, I decided to write one. This book is the result.

This book is mainly concerned with how to achieve imagination skills along with power of imagination and is followed by a demo of landscape painting from imagination.
I hope this book will guide you to understand, how to achieve imagination skills to use in your paintings.

- Magunta Dayakar
  Hyderabad, India

No words of introduction

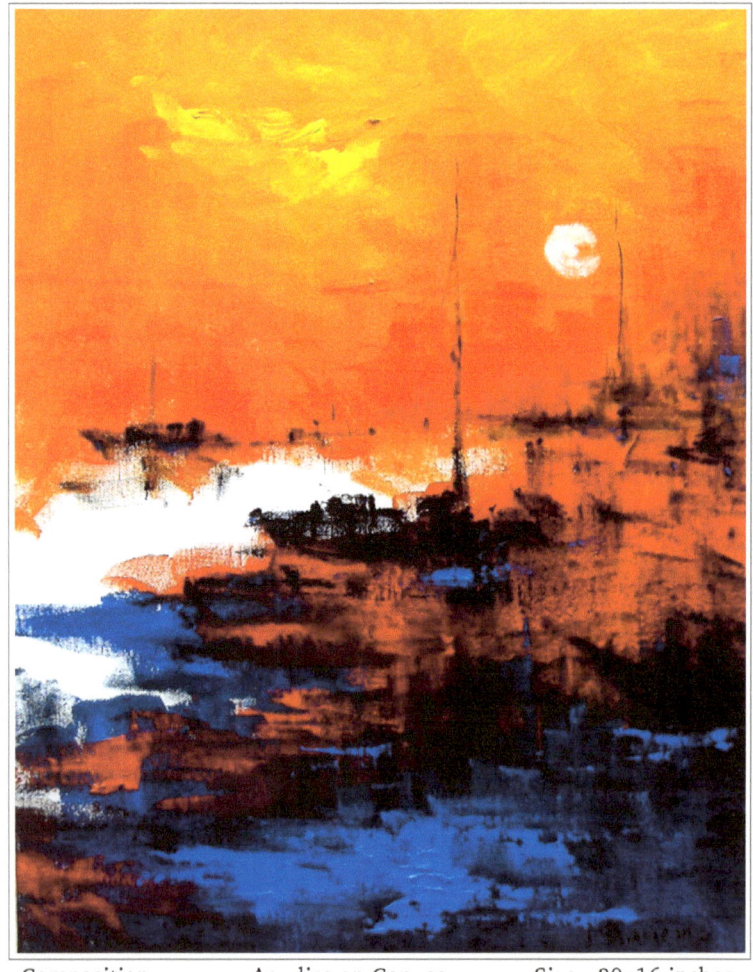

Composition   Acrylics on Canvas   Size : 20x16 inches
Artist : Magunta Dayakar

There will be no introduction words from me about landscape painting. Every art student knows what it is. It is painting a small or a large portion of Nature on canvas. This we call Landscape Painting.

But there are many questions ...Working in plein air, Working in studio from outdoor sketches, Working from photos or Working from Imagination. Which is the right approach? Here are the answers ...

Working in plein air

If you work in plein air, your painting will have movement and color freshness. Reason for this is, you have to work from a scene which extends for a couple of miles or from a smaller part of it on your small canvas which is usually of size one or one and half feet. So to capture that large area on your small canvas, first thing you have to ignore is details. You have to paint only large and medium shapes first instead of details. This act itself brings some life into a painting and it also leads to movement. This movement helps to avoid static feeling. Static feeling means lifelessness.

Next... color. Why do plein air paintings have some color freshness even if they are painted by amateurs? Usually color will lose its freshness by over mixing with other colors. In studio, you have plenty of time to mix colors so if you over do a little bit of it, it causes muddiness. That means losing freshness of color. In plein air it won't happen. The reason ... you won't have much time to work in outdoors like in studio. And with every hour direction of light changes, sometimes fast moving winds, heat, dust, unexpected rains along with many unforeseen problems will push you to do the things quickly. So you have to come to a quick judgement about shapes and colors in nature. Then you don't have much time to make your colors muddy.

Result ... your colors will appear more fresh on the canvas. Loose brush strokes, color freshness and less details, you will get them in plein air even if you are just a beginner.

Working in the studio from outdoor sketches
This will be a big problem if you don't have the right knowledge about value, color and composition. I told you already that when you work in outdoors, your work will have some plus points even if you are an amateur artist but when you want to develop them into finished paintings, there the problem starts.

Now you will have leisure time on your hands, you have a comfortable environment where you won't face any disturbance such as fast moving winds, changing light etc .... How nice it is! You will think that you can work more comfortably in that environment than in outdoors. In fact the problem will start from that moment.

Problem one ... Now you have plenty of time to work your picture so you will try to find where you can add detail. Result - More detail leads to static feel. Problem two ... You will try to mix different color tints and greys and you will paint them on your picture. Result - More color mixtures leads to muddiness and losing freshness of color. Problem three ... loosing of loose brush strokes. Result - This also creates static appearance.

Now you may ask me, there are many artists who work in their studios using outdoor sketches and photographs, what about them?

Yes. Many artists work that way. But all of them have a good understanding about value, color and composition which are the keys to do a successful painting. If you have knowledge like them you can also work from your studio by using reference.

Note this, If you understand value, color and composition along with a few more elements, definitely
you can also work from your studio.

Working from Photos
For a student working from photos is not a wise thing. In photos darks will become more dark. So you are not able to judge color of dark. Darks are transparent, you won't be able to see that transparent nature in photos. And other problem with photos is, they are condensed images of the vast nature. When you see the images of nature in small size print, like 8x10 inches … just imagine, what is there for you to see! Nothing. Those small photo prints will deceive you about the true essence of nature. So, note this... without understanding nature and its wholeness working from photos will be hopeless. You may ask me ..."
Then is it not possible to work from photos? "
Sure, You can work from photos but before that, you must understand mother nature. Observe it, analyse it, imprint the images in your heart, then you can use photos. In this approach those photos will only become a source. You are not painting from them, you are using them for inspiration. This is one part of doing a painting, along with this there is another part, you need to study to create a powerful painting. That is the technical

aspect. That technical aspect involves Value, Color, Composition and a few more elements of art. In coming pages, I will discuss about these.

Working from Imagination

This is the other approach apart from the remaining three. This is the most powerful and effective approach if you are able to work with this. In this book I am going to talk about this approach.

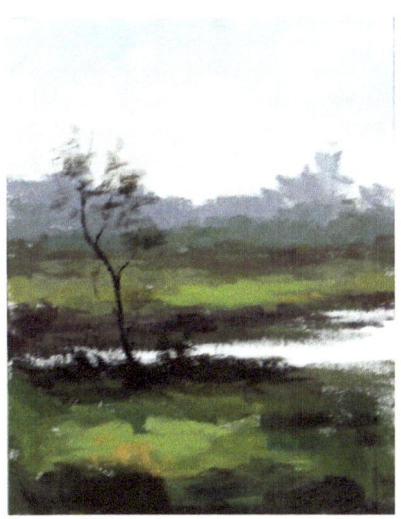
I painted this in outdoors

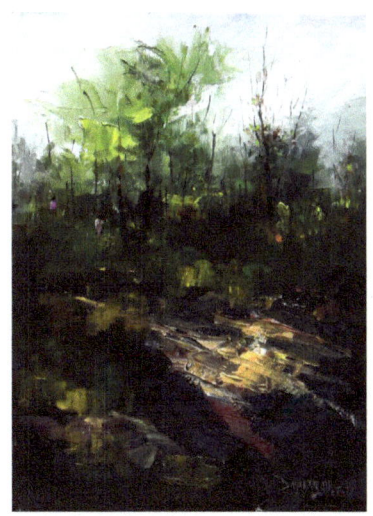
This is also painted in outdoors

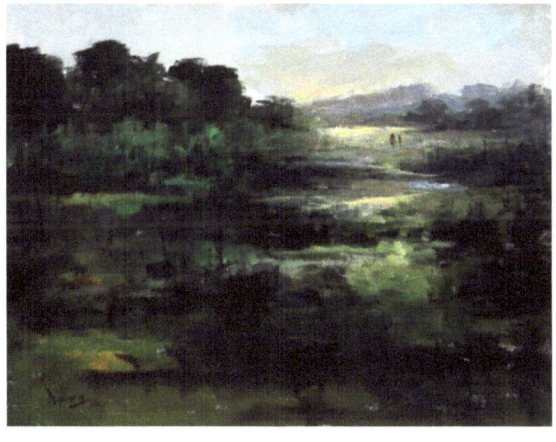

First I painted this in outdoors and later finished it in studio from memory.

Imagination

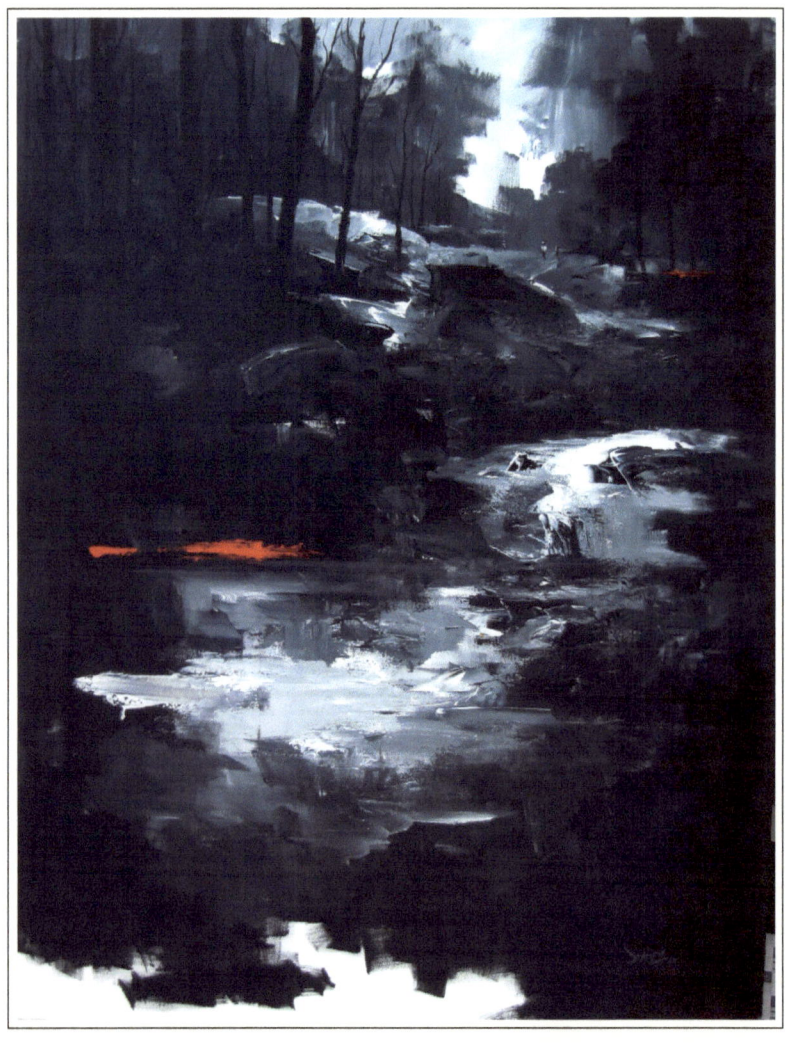

Countryside   Acrylics on Canvas   70x54 inches
Artist : Magunta Dayakar

Imagination. Everyone talks about it without knowing ...what it is!

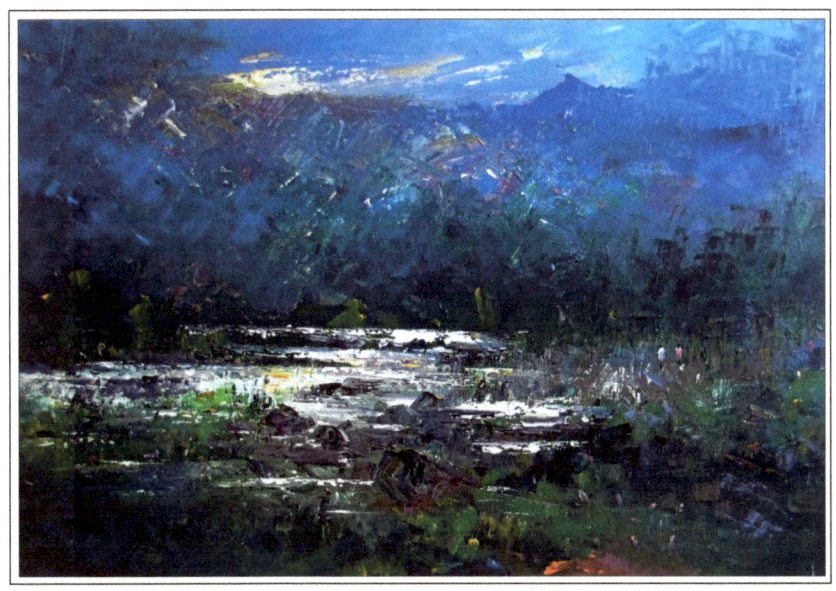

At The Hills   Acrylics on Canvas   Size : 48x36 inches
Artist : Magunta Dayakar

Imagination ... What is it?

Many people talk about this. So many myths, so many wrong notions. I don't want to go into all those theories and arguments. Here I would like to limit myself only to how to paint landscapes from imagination.

For the last few years, I have been doing paintings only from imagination. People used to ask me often, how do you paint these? One of my clients also asked me the same question, " How do you paint these? Do you use photographs for reference?"
" No, I paint them from imagination." I answered her.

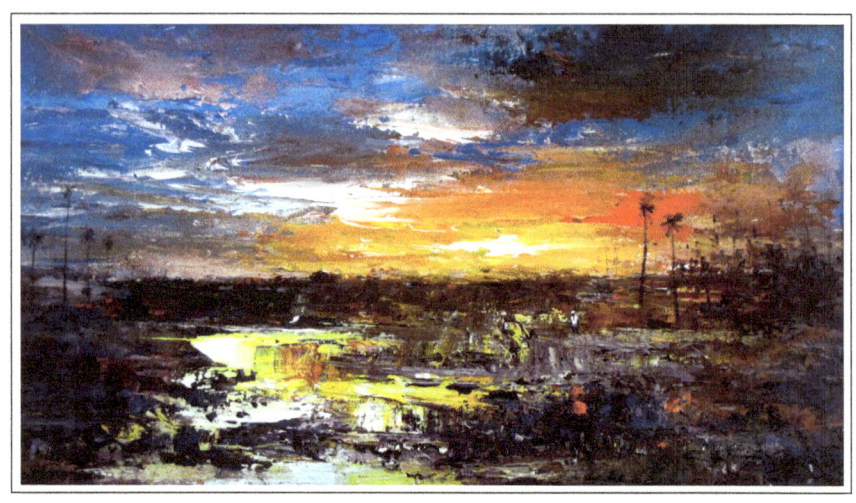

Evening   Acrylics on Canvas   Size : 36x20 inches
Artist : Magunta Dayakar

From Imagination ...

" From imagination …!? " Full of surprise in her voice. " I cannot believe this. They are looking damn realistic, how is it possible to work such realistic works from imagination? "
A slight smile on my face. I didn't comment immediately. Her question is ringing inside me. *" ...how is it possible to work such realistic works from imagination? "*

What a wrong notion people have? Why are they thinking that proper realistic paintings cannot be created from imagination? What things prompted them to think like that?
To answer her questions first I have to talk about imagination.

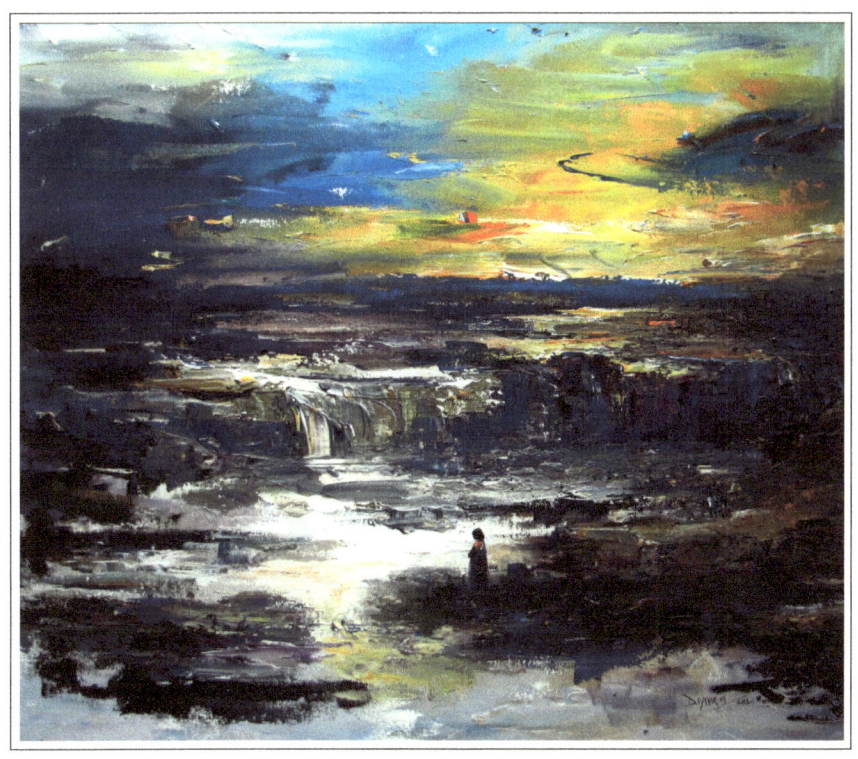

Waiting   Acrylics on Canvas   Size : 60x44 inches
Artist : Magunta Dayakar

How do you know ...

" Tell me what do you know about imagination? " I asked her.
She looked at me with a confused expression.
I know her confusion and her state of mind in that moment.
People talk so much about imagination. But in fact they don't know exactly what it is. Just they talk about it in general. Few years ago, a lady came to me to join her child in my art school. That child was five years old.
That lady said to me, " Sir, my child has very good imagination

skills..."

I used to listen to these kind of statements often. I paused for a moment and then asked her, " How do you know that your child has very good imagination skills?"

She fell into silence, searching for an answer. After few moments of silence she said, " she will draw many things without copying anything, like buses, cars, trees, huts, hills, sun, moon.... is it not imagination? "

I smiled and said ..." No. It's not imagination. She is drawing them from memory."

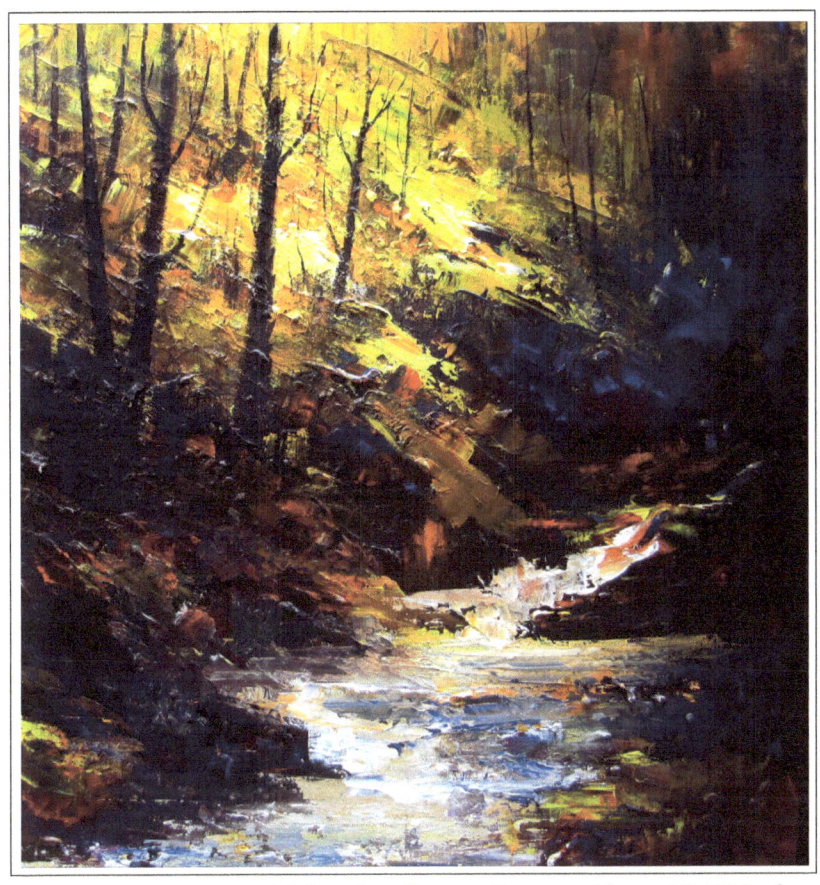

Light   Acrylics on Canvas   Size : 36x30 inches
Artist : Magunta Dayakar

I know it always happens ...

" I don't understand … I think it is imagination but you are saying it's memory! "
I know, it always happens like that. In general most of the people don't distinguish between memory and imagination. I told her, " Memory and imagination both are two different

things. Memory is one of the parts of imagination."
She had become a little bit angry. It showed on her face. Then she asked me, " Do you mean my child doesn't have imagination skills? "
" She has a part of it …" I said.
" I don't understand sir "
I looked at her for a moment and said … " Yes. Memory is one of the parts of imagination."
" … you mean imagination consists of some parts? " she asked me with surprise.
I nodded and smiled at her.

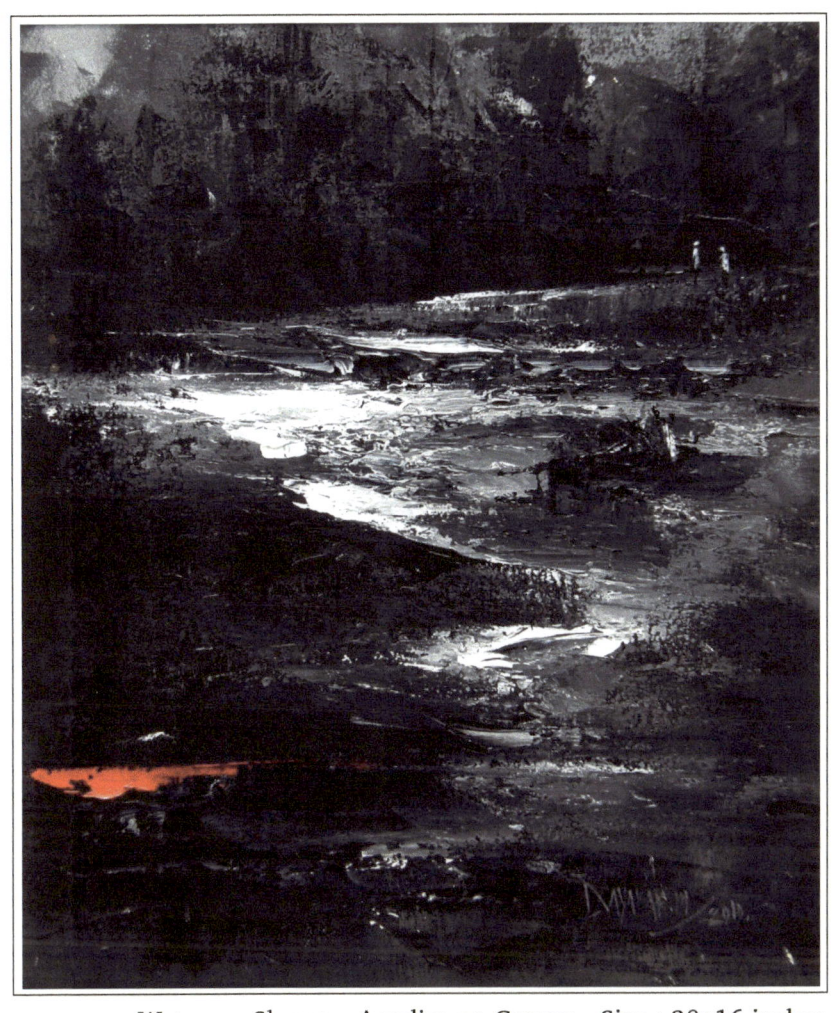

Water on Slopes   Acrylics on Canvas   Size : 20x16 inches
Artist : Magunta Dayakar

Those Three ...

" Imagination consists of three parts " I started to tell her,
" observation, concentration and memory, these three parts will

lead to imagination. The one who is good at those three will achieve imagination skills. "

" Can you explain me more..."

" Sure. It starts with observation..."

"...Observation? "

" Yes. It's the starting point for imagination. That's why there is a saying ... Observation is the key to Drawing. That means to draw well you need good observation skills."

" ... Interesting! "

" Yes. Observation is the key to drawing. What is drawing? Drawing is nothing but using only a line and a curve. You should acquire the ability of using this line and curve to create different shapes and sizes. That means you have to understand shapes and sizes of things. This is seeing the things as an artist. We call it...learning to see. This is Observation."

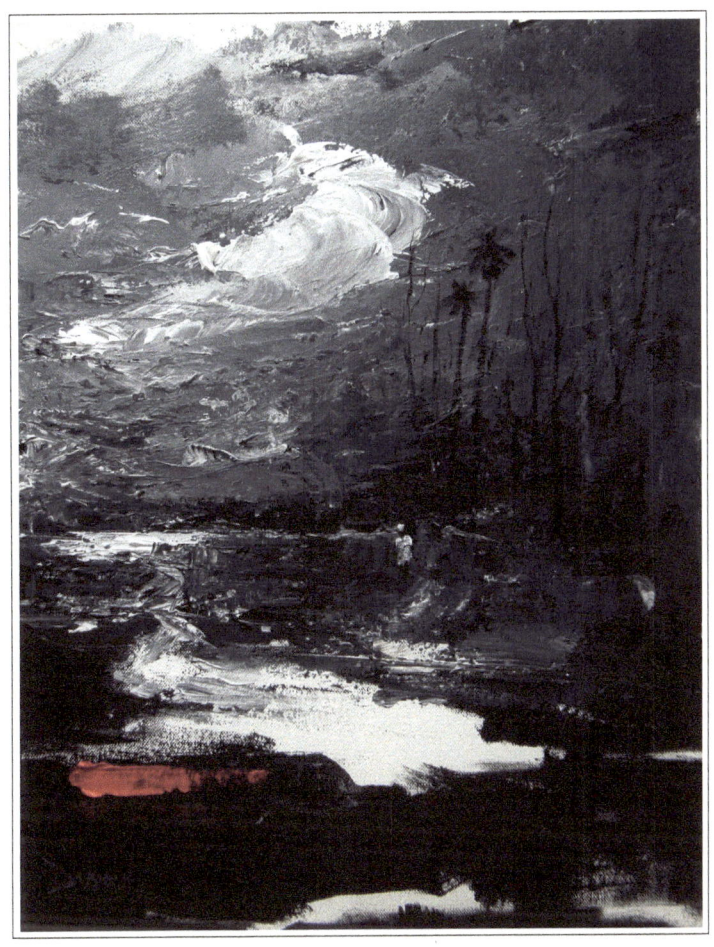

The Cloud   Acrylics on Canvas   Size : 18x14 inches
Artist : Magunta Dayakar

Observation ... how it works?

Sometime back, one incident happened in my class room. One of my students was copying a drawing. After one hour, in the middle of drawing, she understood something had gone wrong.

And she also understood, where it had gone wrong.
She drew one of the shapes in the picture, a little bit big. So all the connected parts with that particular part had gone wrong in their proportions. She lost. I told her again, what I said previously to her...'' Don't draw. Look at it. Judge heights and widths and their relations. It will come.''
She had started to work again. This time she began to see their heights, widths and their relations, rather than seeing the picture. Then she got it.

  I asked her…" What went through your mind in the first and second attempts? "
She told me that in her first attempt she concentrated on the picture … how to copy it? In her second attempt, she did not bother about copying the picture. She concentrated only on heights and widths of the shapes and their relations. This is what she said.

 I narrated that incident to the lady who sat in front of me. She was silent for a few moments, thinking seriously about my words ...

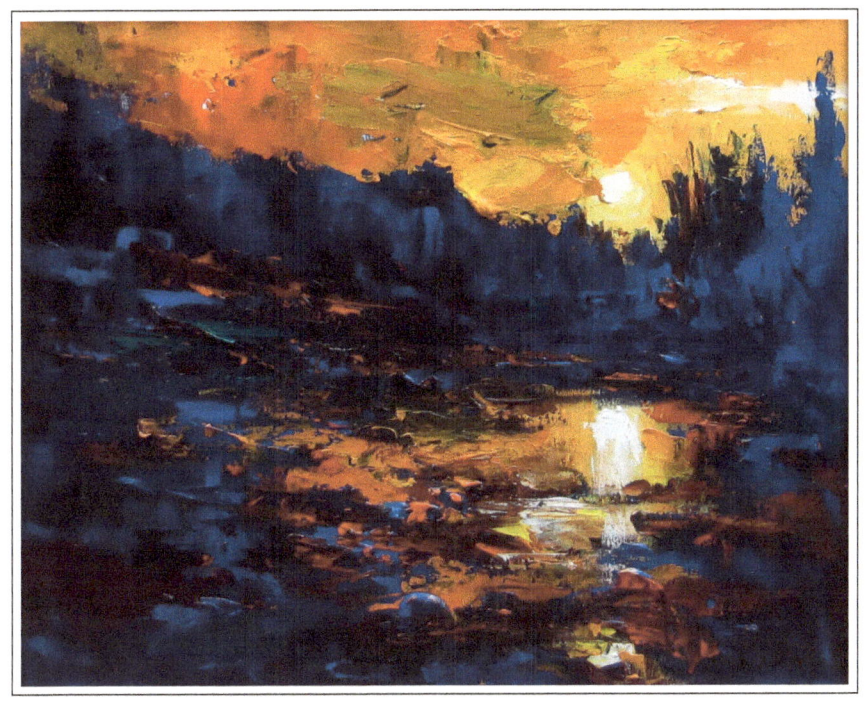

Sunset   Acrylics on Canvas   Size : 30x24 inches
Artist ; Magunta Dayakar

Relations ...

After some time she said, " So she observed the relations between the lines and between the shapes."
"Yes"
" That's fine, but … how is it related to imagination?"
I liked that question, it brought a smile to my lips. I told her, "
"In this world and in our lives everything is connected to everything. That you call … relation. These relations can be understood by observation. Observation is not just seeing the

thing without thinking. Here thinking is the key. You are observing means you are thinking. You are analysing the relations between the elements in the picture … you are thinking about its structure, you are thinking about light which falls there, you are seeing the textures in the light and color … this is observation. Observation with thinking. "

" I have understood through your words that thinking is the key to Observation " So much curiosity in her.

I nodded. " Yes. It is. Observation with thinking … either way. I will tell you one of my experiences... " Sometime back I had been observing sunset for some time every day at the same hour. One day after sunset, I went to my studio like any other day. But something happened in me. In my studio, in the dark, in between four walls, I had begun seeing the sunset through my mind's eye, it was as if I was standing before a sunset. How did it happen? Is it just because of observation? No. Only observation is not enough. Observation should be accompanied with thought process."

" Thought process! What is it? "

" Already I told you, observation with thinking. In fact, thinking is a part of observation. Without thinking there is no observation, it's just looking at the things. When you are passing on the road you are seeing many things whatever comes your way. Just you are seeing them, you are not thinking about them, you are not analysing them, you are not interpreting them, you are not responding to them emotionally, it's just seeing like a moving camera which is not having film. You call this … Looking at things. This looking is no way connected to observation. Observation means analysing, interpreting and responding emotionally.

This was what happened with me when I was observing that sunset. The sun light, its reflections in the water, the tree rows between water and sky, their purple colors, warm orange and purple colors in the sky, ground textures …. everything I observed, everything I analysed, interpreted, connected with them emotionally ... In the end I painted the whole scene on my heart, in the process I turned my heart as my canvas, my eyes and mind became brushes and tools." I stopped talking, slipping into the memories of that sunset.

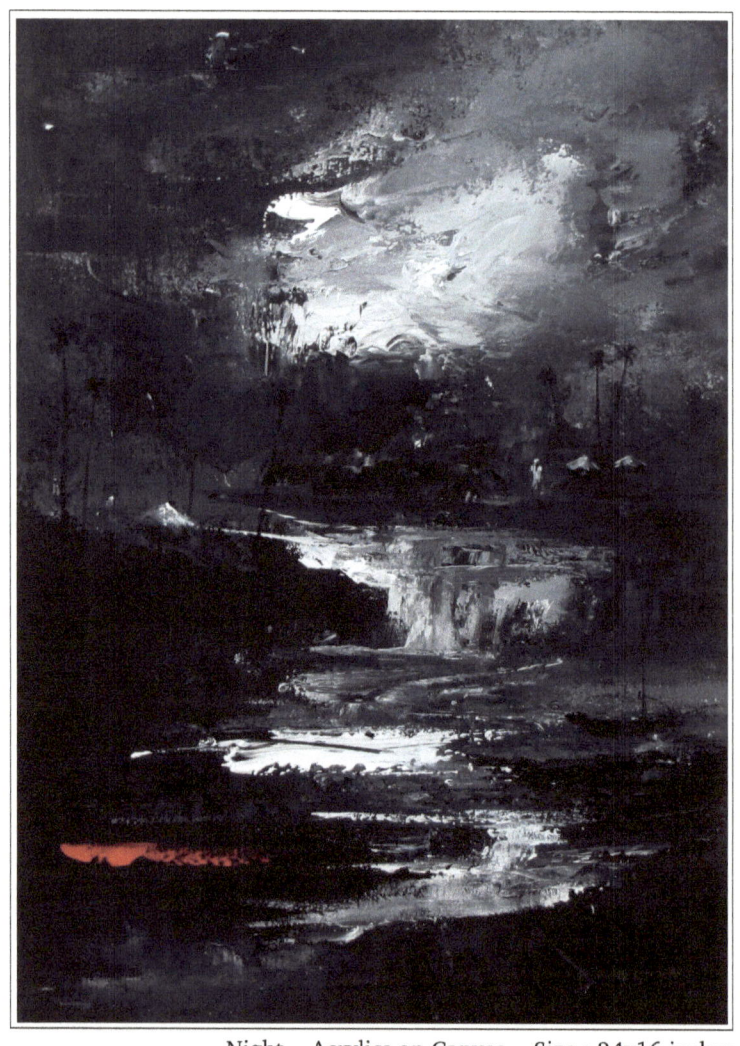

Night   Acrylics on Canvas   Size : 24x16 inches
Artist ; Magunta Dayakar

It's the same here

A few minutes of silence, she was observing me.
Then she said, "So continuous Observation with thinking leads

to the picture becoming a part of you"
"Okay, then what about concentration? "

I replied," You don't need to bother to train to practice concentration. When you are in the act of observation, automatically you will be in concentration. The act itself is concentration. It's like second skin.
" What you are saying is, If we observe the scene with thinking process, concentration will come naturally, without trying for it? "
" … Exactly."
Again she became silent, lost in thought.
After some time she said, " I have understood what you said. One more thing … "
Looking at her, I am waiting for the question.
" … you told me imagination consists of three parts. You have explained observation and concentration, what about the third part memory? Where does it fit here? "
" Like concentration, memory also happens automatically. When you are observing, analysing, interpreting and responding to a scene or a thing those images will get imprinted in your mind. They will be there forever. They would be never erased from your mind. You must understand one crucial thing in this process. What you have received into your memory is not done by conscious effort. It happened through your emotional response just like your childhood sweet memories which you never forget in your life. It's the same here.

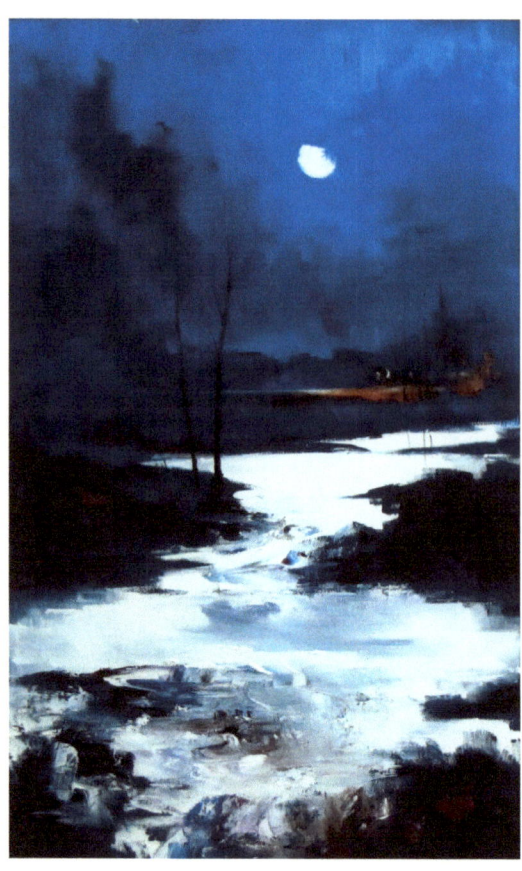

The Moon   Acrylics on Canvas
Size : 60x33 inches
Artist : Magunta Dayakar

Then how do you say ...

" One thing I am not understanding properly ... I don't think what you described is imagination." she said.
I had been looking at her to know what she was going to say.
" ... you told me that you have observed a scene with thinking, concentration follows, finally it stands in your memory, you painted it. That means you painted it from memory, you said

memory is only a part of imagination. Then how do you say you painted that sunset from imagination? "
I smiled and then replied.
" … you didn't get the total picture, there is some thing more you should know about observation. This act of observation won't be limited to one visual or one scene to paint a picture. You have to observe infinite images like that. It's a continuous process. With time you will have a lot of images in your heart through emotional responses. That will become a huge library of images in you. When you start to paint from imagination a number of images from that library will move on the emotional screen of your heart. Through your experience and taste you may choose some of them. It's like sky from one image, foreground from another image, water from another source... its infinite. You can choose hundreds of images from the library which exists in your heart. Why it is heart? Why not the mind? Mind will memorise whereas heart will experience them, own them, those feelings and responses would stay as your second skin.
But this second skin is not enough to make you imaginative. You need composition skills. Because of composition, you will be able to form new structures using those images. Here the key is … forming new structures. It's not possible from memory. Memory will keep the things to certain extent as a part of your mind whereas experiences become a part of yourself.
See the picture which is given on the next page. Observe it. Study it. Question yourself. Could you see that kind of scene in nature? Not possible, its orchestrated like rhythmic music. The yellow orange sky, its reflection in the shallow water, blue purple trees … everything is selected from the emotional experiences of heart, and connected with Composition. This whole process is called as … Imagination.

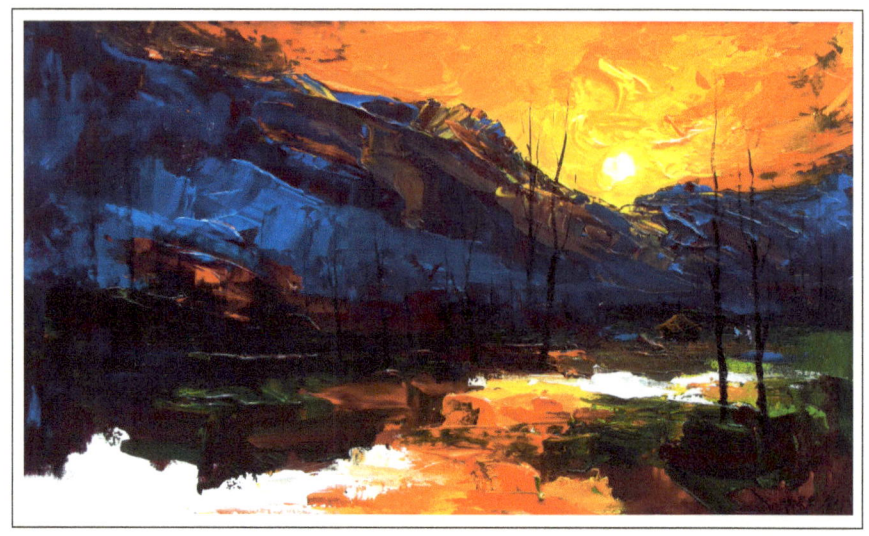

A Hut   Acrylics on Canvas   Size : 30x16 inches
Artist : Magunta Dayakar

(To know about composition in detail please read my book … ' How To Start Painting And How To Plan It ? ')

Summary

Imagination is the combination of many things.

Observation with thinking

It starts with observation and thinking. You are observing means you are thinking. When you are looking at something and at the same time thinking about it, trying to know about it in depth, that act will make you concentrate. You don't need to practice to get concentration. Most of the people try to get concentration through effort as if it's a skill. Don't do that way. Observe and think about it, you are in concentration. Note this … You won't get concentration by any other means.

Next … Memory.

Many people practice different methods to get memory skills. It's a wrong notion. Like concentration, it's not a skill to learn. It has to come to you through your work. It's a very simple process. When you are involved with something intensively you won't forget it. That will stay in you forever. You call this memory. Whatever work you do, do it with total involvement, then it will remain in your memory forever.

Finally … Imagination.

If you make observation and thinking as your second nature, If you put that habit in every moment of your life it will lead to imagination. Without conscious effort you will be able to imagine many things beyond their limits. For an example, if some incident happens, you begin to think about its consequences and where it will lead to next.. next... next... This is imagination. Remember … Imagination comes out of observation and thinking. Structures, situations, relations are the elements of imagination. Analyzing, interpreting and connecting the elements of imagination leads to bringing imagination into reality. In art you call these applications… Composition. Not only in art, this applies to any field.

The Power Of Imagination

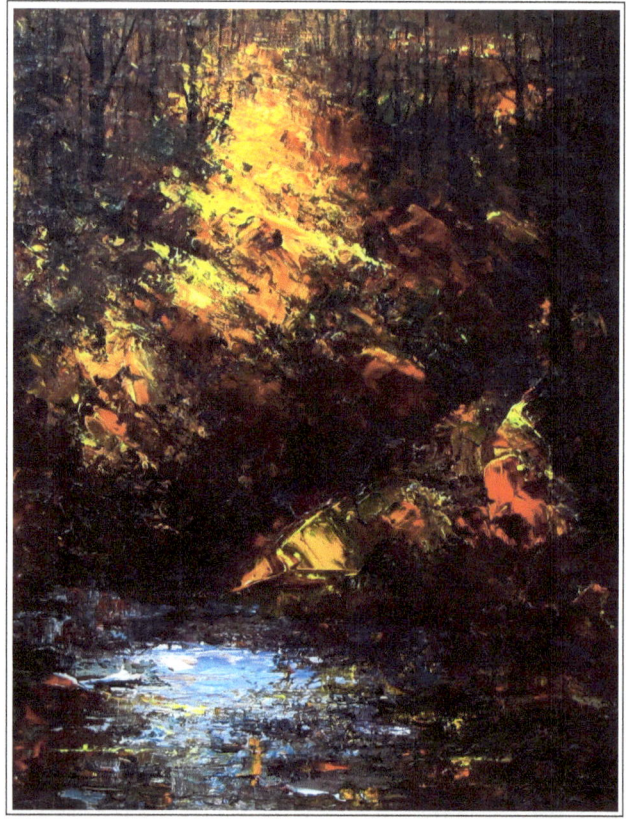

A Small Pond   Acrylics on Canvas   Size : 30x36 inches
Artist : Magunta Dayakar

The act of imagination is very powerful and exciting with its unpredictable and mysterious ways but to get the best effect, you need to use it to its full extent.

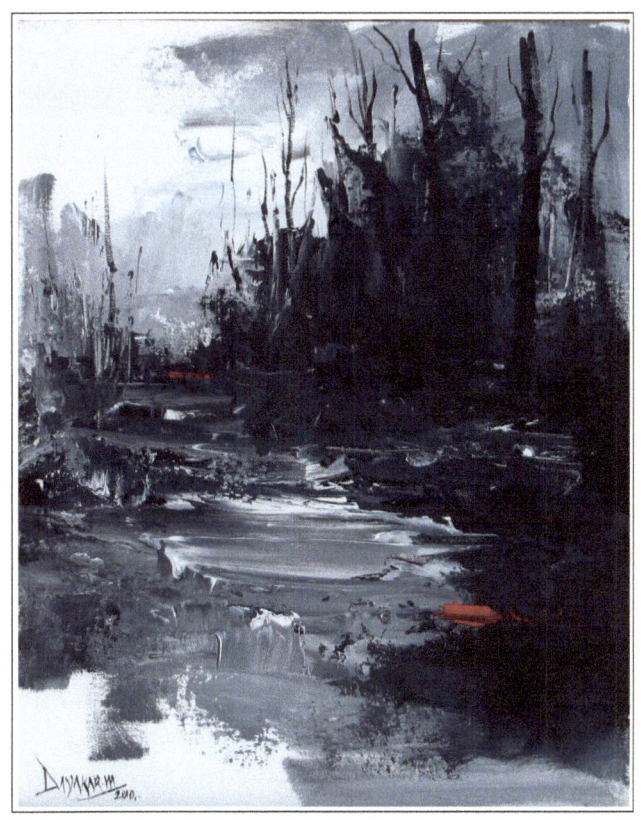

Landscape   Acrylics on Canvas   Size: 18x14 inches
Artist : Magunta Dayakar

Why most of the artists are not successful in this ...

Everything in this universe has its own limits but our imagination has no limits. When you are painting from plein air you paint only what you are seeing.
If you are an experienced artist you may omit some shapes, you may change their sizes or places for composition purpose.
A little bit of color changes you do to suit your color scheme. You can also do value changes related to your focal point.

You could not go beyond this.

If a group of experienced artists paint from the same scene, in the end every one's painting may be different because of ...
their view point
their composition plan
their color scheme
their value key
and finally their taste. That's it.

When a viewer sees all those paintings at once or on different occasions he will enjoy them, he will appreciate their beauty and he will praise the artists' skills for creating such beautiful works.
But ... he feels nothing new, no surprise. He has been seeing that kind of visuals since ages. Just some more beautiful paintings.
Why the viewer thinks like that after seeing such beautiful works?
Reason one ... Every artist worked from the same scene.
Reason two ... Everyone followed the same rules of value, color and composition.
Of course, even though rules are the same every artist applies them differently according to their individual taste but everyone painted the same scene. Problem lies here. For the viewer, in their work there won't be any visual surprise related to nature. Only applications and approaches are differing from artist to artist. Same thing happens when you work in the studio either from photographs or outdoor studies combined with photographs.

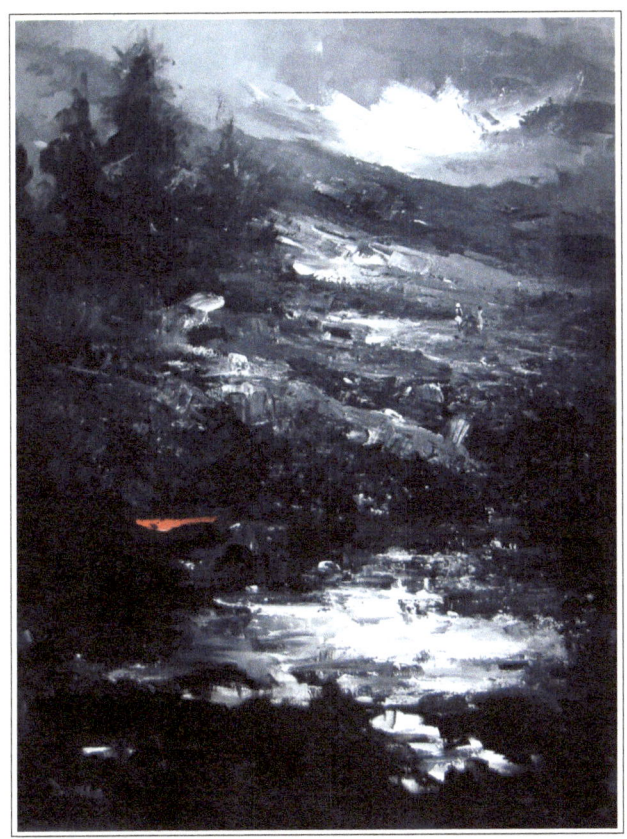

Cloud and Hills   Acrylics on Canvas   Size : 70x54 inches
Artist : Magunta Dayakar

Is this problem happening to all artists of all ages?

I don't think so. This problem started at the end of nineteenth century when the first motion picture was made.
Later it was with the internet.
Before movies were made, people were not able to see the faraway places. If they want to see, they have to go personally to see them which was very troublesome and expensive and to

most of the people this was not possible also. So if they see an artist's painting which depicts the local scene from where the artist lives, it is a new thing for them. It's interesting and sometimes surprising depending upon the artist's skills and taste.

But it is a changed situation now.

We are seeing everything from the nook and corners of the world through movies and videos. We are seeing the virtual museums, we are seeing the city streets, monuments, beautiful tourist spots, people's lives in different countries, the rich, the poor, the beauty and the ugly … everything.

So where is the surprise? How it will come to the people of this age? No way …!

I think due to this reason artist shifted to modern, abstract and other forms of art. But ordinary people are not able to grasp them so no response, no surprise. Because of this, those different forms of art are connected only with rich and privileged people of the society. No one knows how much they actually respond to in their inside to these new forms of art. Only they can say. Anyway, in this process, art itself got distanced from the majority of the society. So art and artist have become isolated from the ordinary people.

To earn money for survival you need wealthy people but for inspiration you need ordinary people. If they respond to your work they will appreciate you tremendously. There won't be any limits. Just they put out everything they feel. As an artist you will be excited by their emotional expression. It will inspire you to work more. With wealthy people, usually it won't happen like that. Due to their habits most of them won't come out with their feelings in the open.

As an artist you need both … inspiration and money. To achieve that you need to surprise people of all sections in the society. Working from Imagination is the key to that.

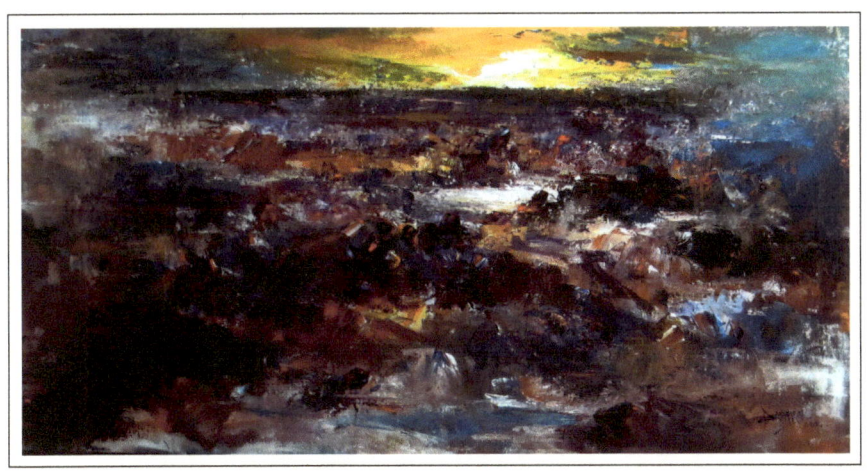

Horizon   Acrylics on Canvas   Size : 40x22 inches
Artist : Magunta Dayakar

How it happens from imagination?

Imagination has no limits. You can travel anywhere in this universe or you can create your own universe. You can see anything in your mind's eye whether they are trees, skies, water, mountains, city streets, rural roads, countryside or any other thing. No boundaries. You can get whatever light into your work, you can bring whatever atmosphere you like to show in your painting and finally you can create ... your world. You are the master. Your work will surprise all whether they are elite or ordinary.

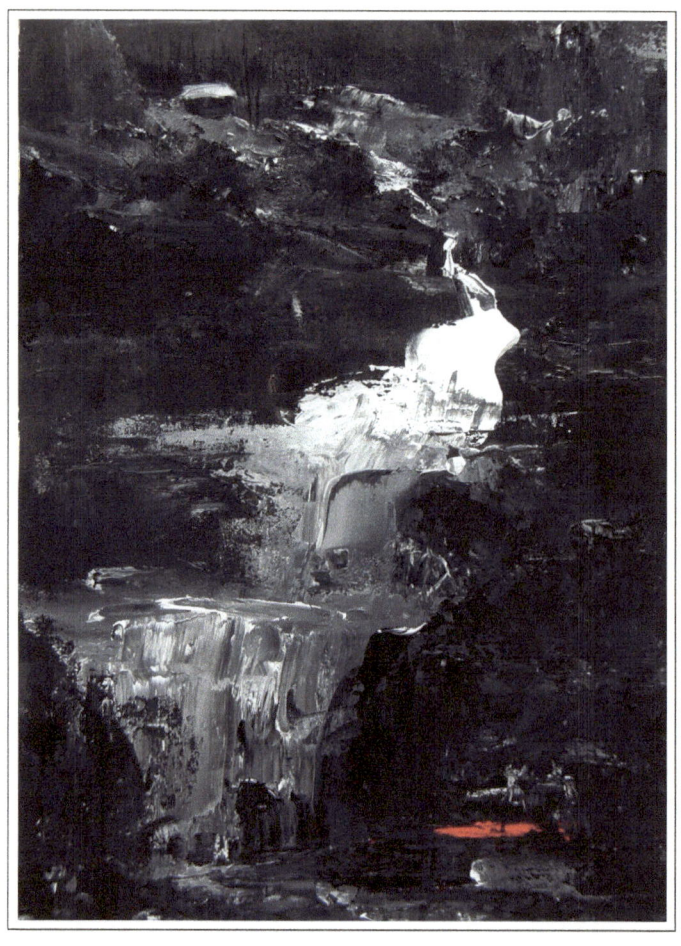

From The Top   Acrylics on Canvas   Size : 20x14 inches
Artist : Magunta Dayakar

But you must learn ….

If you are working from imagination, you don't need to bother about working conditions of outdoor nor do you need to worry about the quality of reference sources to work in the studio. Just

it is you and your studio.
But story does not end here.
Whatever imagination skills you will achieve, to make them work on canvas, you must learn about the elements of art, principles of composition. You call them as Science of Painting. This subject involves Value, Color, Composition and a few more things. These things will help you to structure the painting. If you want to paint good ones you have to learn them. If you want to paint from imagination you must know them because you have to create everything through your mind's eye. Nothing is in front of you but you have to structure them with balance, harmony and unity. Knowing the elements of art and principles of composition will help you to turn your imagination into reality on your canvas.
(I have written about Value, Color and Composition in my book ' How To Start A Painting And How to Plan it?)

Demo

Painting from Imagination - Demo

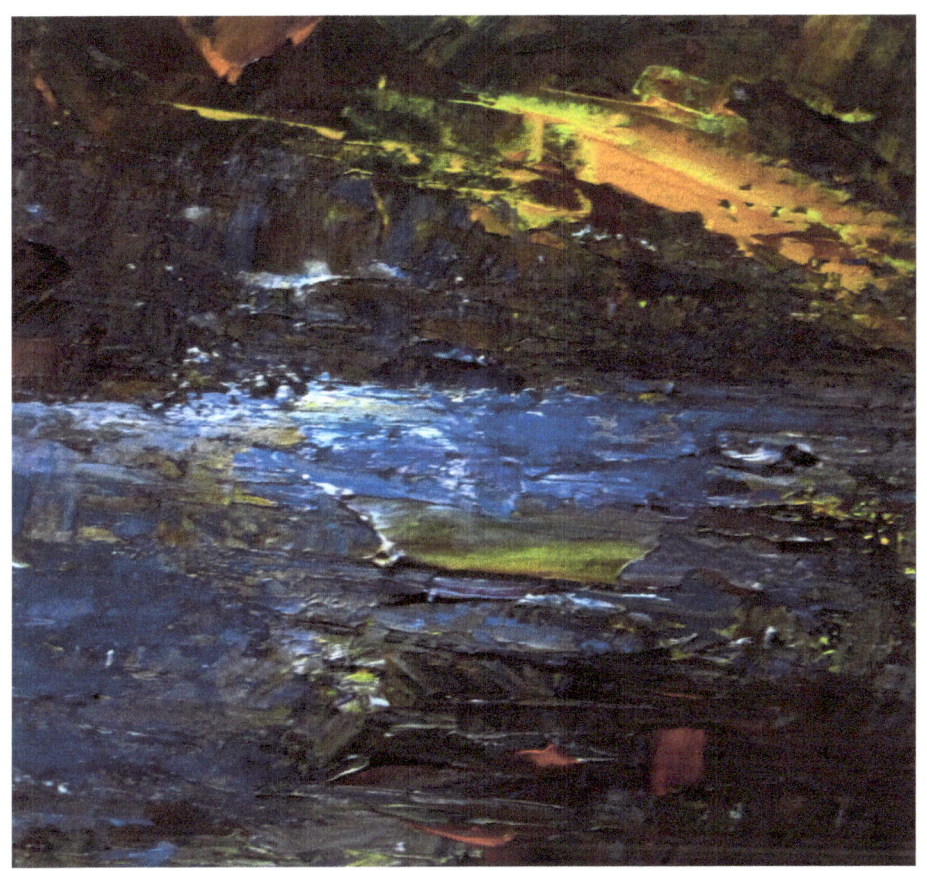

Someone told me " I would like to do a good painting."
" To know what is good, first learn elements of art and principles of composition. " I told him.

In next few pages I am giving a demo about how I start and finish a painting from imagination ...

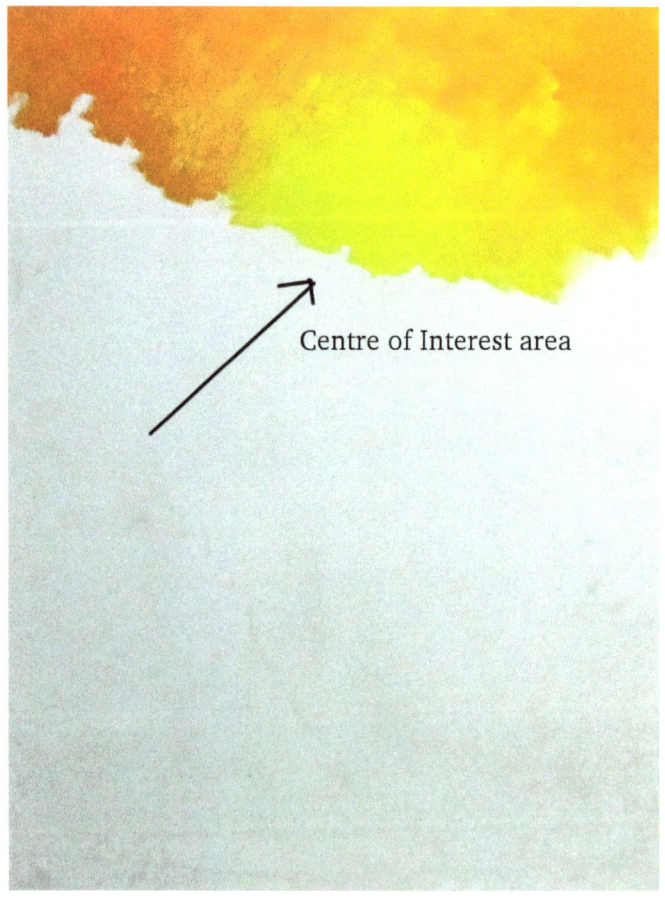

When I do paintings from imagination (Except portraits, for the last few years I have been doing paintings only from imagination), I will start with my centre of interest area where I place highest light. Starting from that, I will move to other places. Here also I started with centre of interest by using lemon yellow and deep yellow.

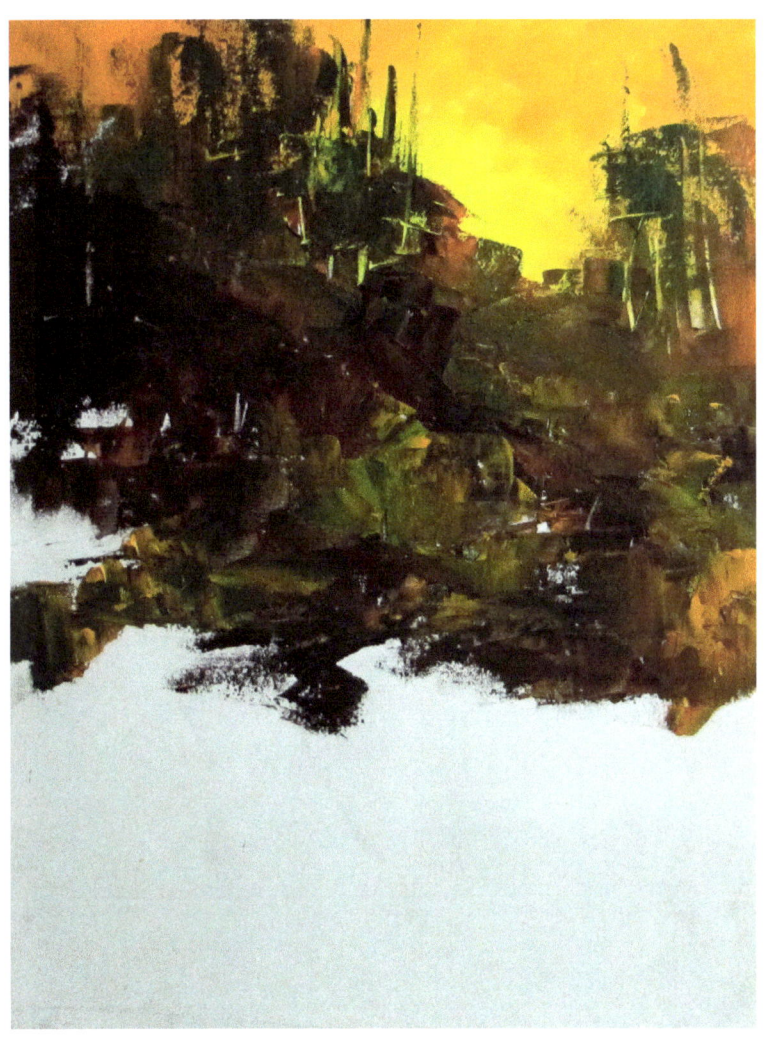

After painting centre of interest, I added some slopes which usually exist on hills. With knife I worked those areas using deep yellow, orange, sap green and deep magenta.
Here I used overlap approach. Overlap approach means,

covering the distant one with next nearest one. For example, sky is the distant one, hills will come next, after that it would be middle ground, finally it's foreground. Paint the verticals in the end. Usually those verticals will be trees, buildings, people etc. When you paint a landscape, the better approach is to keep things simple.

Why is it a better approach?

In nature we see the things that way. We will see the sky, hills, middle ground and foreground in that sequence. When we are painting a landscape if we follow this sequence the painting appears natural.

Many art students think, working in detail will make their painting appear natural and realistic. It's not true. In fact it will make the painting artificial. You should paint the way your eye will see it. That will look realistic.

Spend some time to study how your eye will see the things or nature or people or whatever the subject may be.

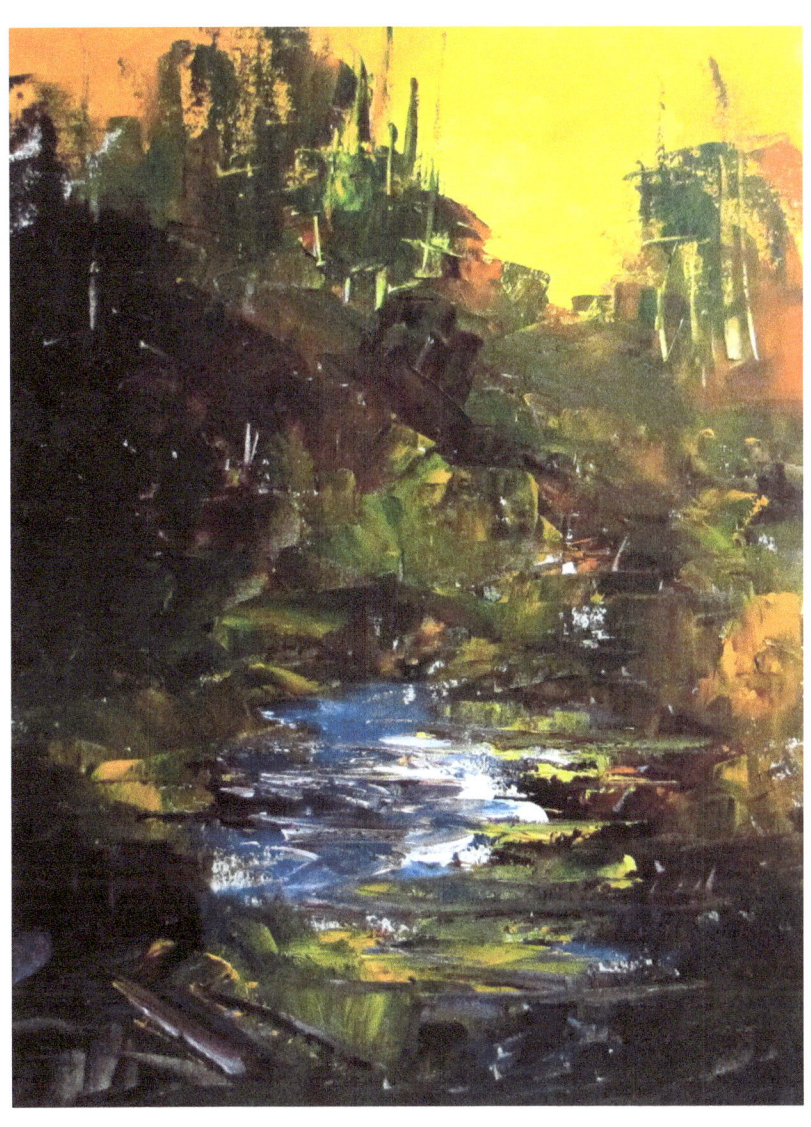

I painted the foreground with a small pond. I used a little bit of ultramarine blue along with remaining colors. With this I structured overall painting. Now I have a scene in front of me on my canvas.

I didn't use any reference for this. Just it's a play with value, color and composition. In fact, it's a highly exciting play. You don't know what's going to happen next. Everything is unpredictable.

This unpredictability is the key to the successful journey of an artist. Why? Just imagine or think... When you are travelling to an unknown destination, everything is ambiguous, mysterious, you don't know what's going to happen next or at the end. Every moment is unpredictable. Anything may happen at any moment. The thought itself will make you tense. You will become anxious but you are continuing the journey, there is no return. Imagine, your state of mind.

Painting from imagination is also like that. You have no reference, no resource, no model, no plein air location. Nothing. You have to imagine everything in your mind. You have to see through your painter's eye. Why with painter's eye you have to see it? What is painter's eye? It is the combination of intuition and technical skills.

Okay. Coming to the previous image ... Why did I put the pond in the foreground? It's for variety. Variety is one of the tools of composition. If I paint total slope on picture space it may be boring at this stage. It needs something other than slope. A pond is a good idea. Earth and water they are connected always with each other yet they are different. One is hard whereas other one is fluid. This difference gives variety.

And putting a pond gives me color difference also. I used yellow, yellow orange predominantly in the painting, blue violet will work as a complementary color for it. Ultramarine blue is suited for that. This thought made me to paint that pond there.

One thing you must remember ... knowledgeable artists won't paint unnecessary shapes and brush strokes. The try to find a relation in everything.

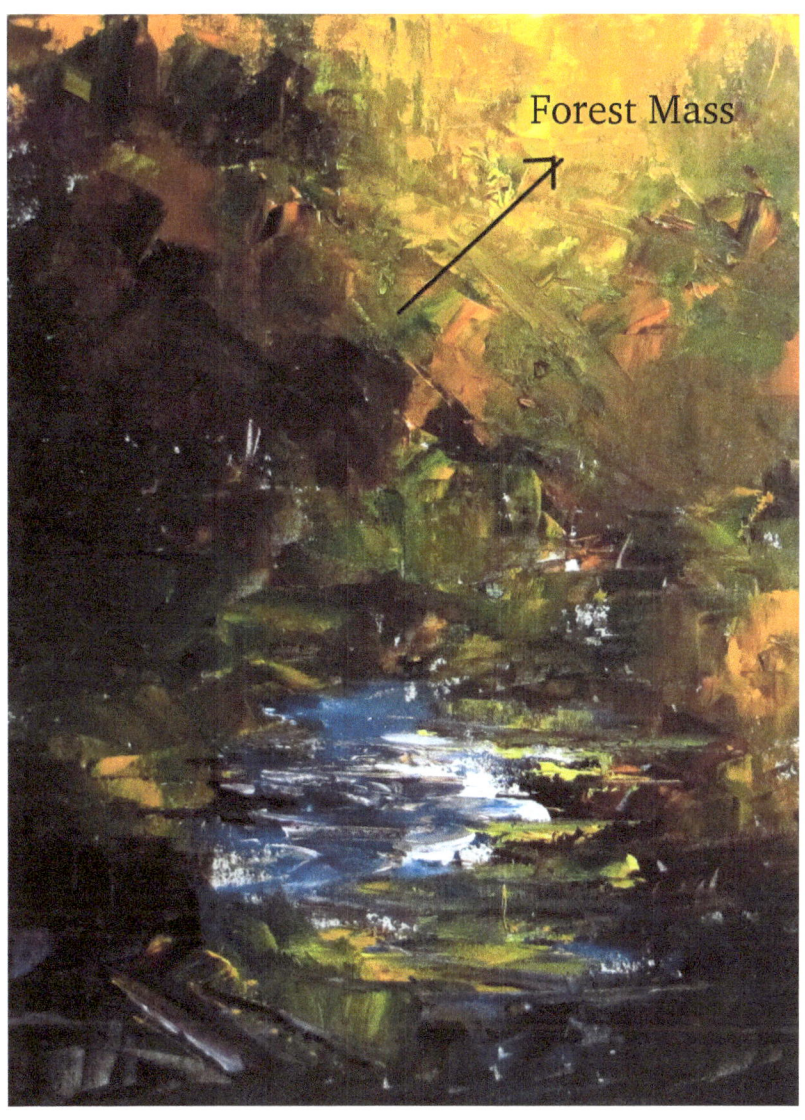

At Every stage, at every moment I used to observe what I have done on the picture space. It's a must. Because you are not copying or replicating or using some source to create a part of nature on your canvas. It's just your imagination, you are creating everything from imagination. Harmony is a very important outcome of composition, it will come through proper relations of shapes, spaces, values, colours and many more things.

After observing for some time, what I painted, I decided to replace the sky with forest masses.

Why forest masses? What are they?

Inside of the forest you can see the slopes. Some slopes remain simply flat without any trees but somewhere at the end you can see the trees, thin, thick, tall, small, ups and downs... they are forest masses.

When you see those masses from distance they will evoke many feelings in you. You don't know what lies inside of those masses. They are mysterious.

I want to create that mystery in my painting by replacing the sky with forest masses. So I did that.

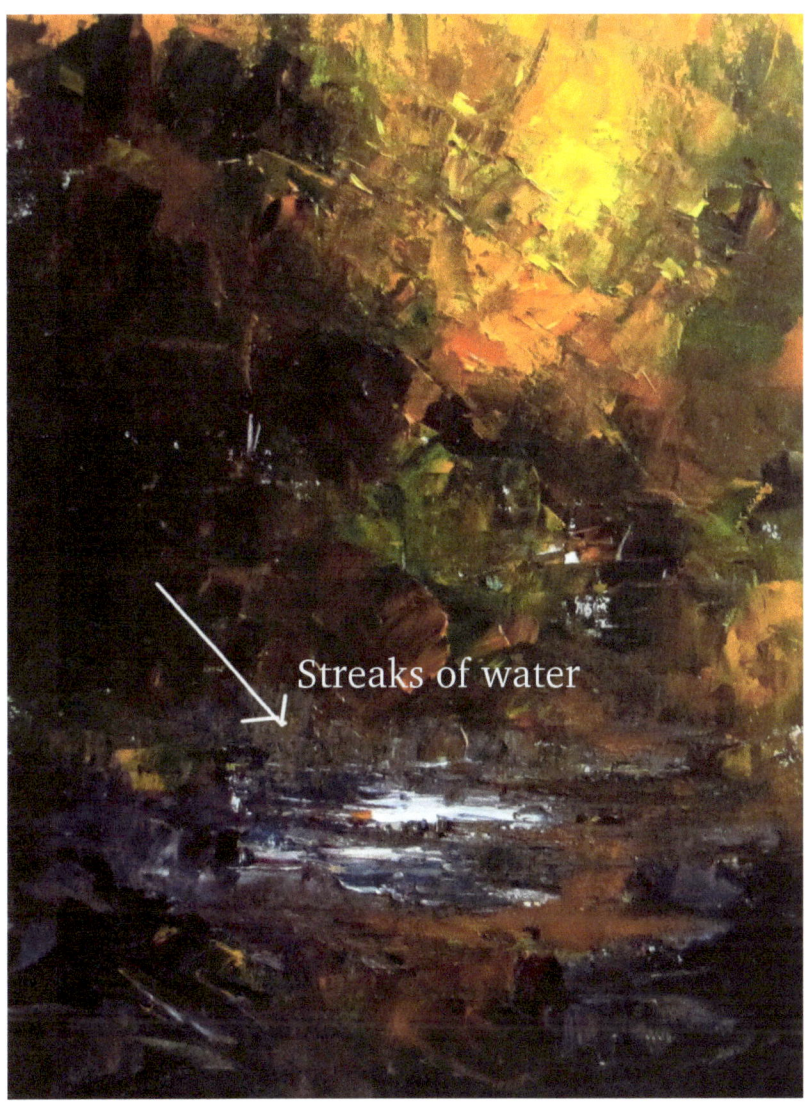

Here I changed the pond into a few streaks of water. I thought, in that terrain, few streaks of water will be better rather than having a pond. And also I refined the area of forest masses, of course, its my centre of interest also.

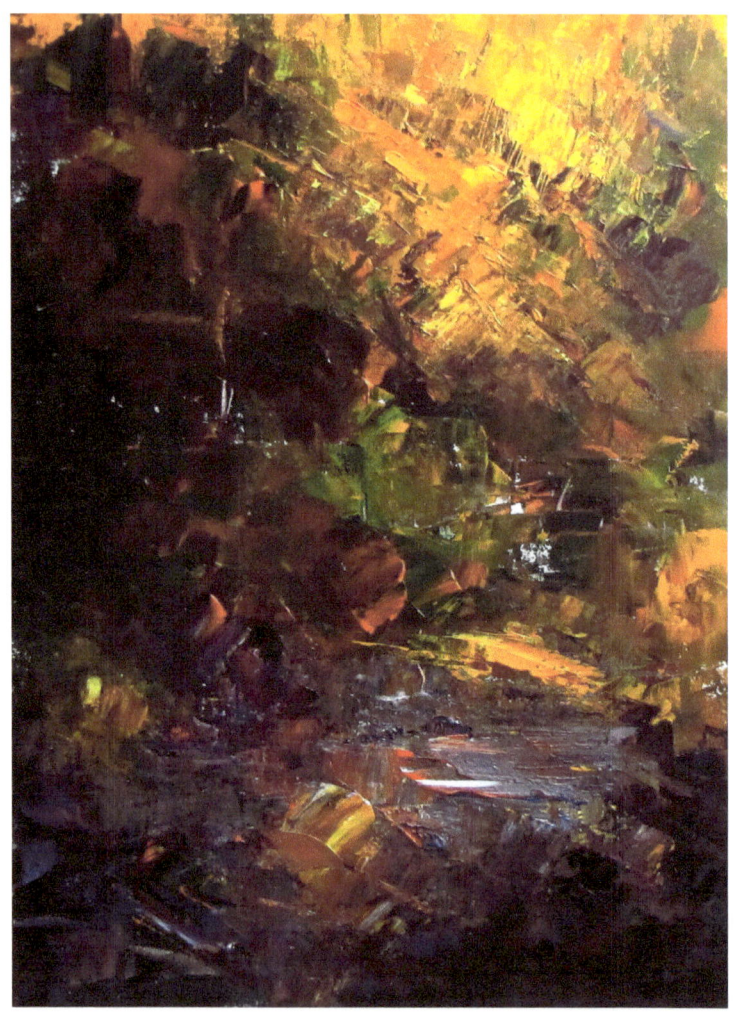

Even though the streaks of water were beautiful I didn't feel good. Something went wrong. I have understood why it's gone wrong.
Just observe the water streaks in the previous picture. When you see the painting, your eye will stay for a few moments on the water, only then it moves up.

I don't want that kind of visual moment from the viewer. I would like to make him to move his eye from bottom to top where the highest light lies without long stops in between. That highest light is ... my centre of interest.

After staying sometime at the centre of interest, then only his eyes have to move from that place to see the remaining picture. You call this ... visual movement of the viewer. Every artist will plan this visual movement in his painting.

So I changed those water streaks into a single streak of water. Now viewer's eye won't stay much time there. It will see it, will stay for a moment, then it will move upwards. And at the same moment that white streak will work as a balance for the upper masses in the picture space. This is what I want. And I refined some more of the centre of interest area.

My son asked me ..." Those water streaks are beautiful. Why did you remove them?"

I said..." Yes. They are beautiful but for my planning they were not suitable. To get what we want, sometimes we have to sacrifice good things too."

If you don't have this kind of ruthless nature, you would not be able to paint from imagination.

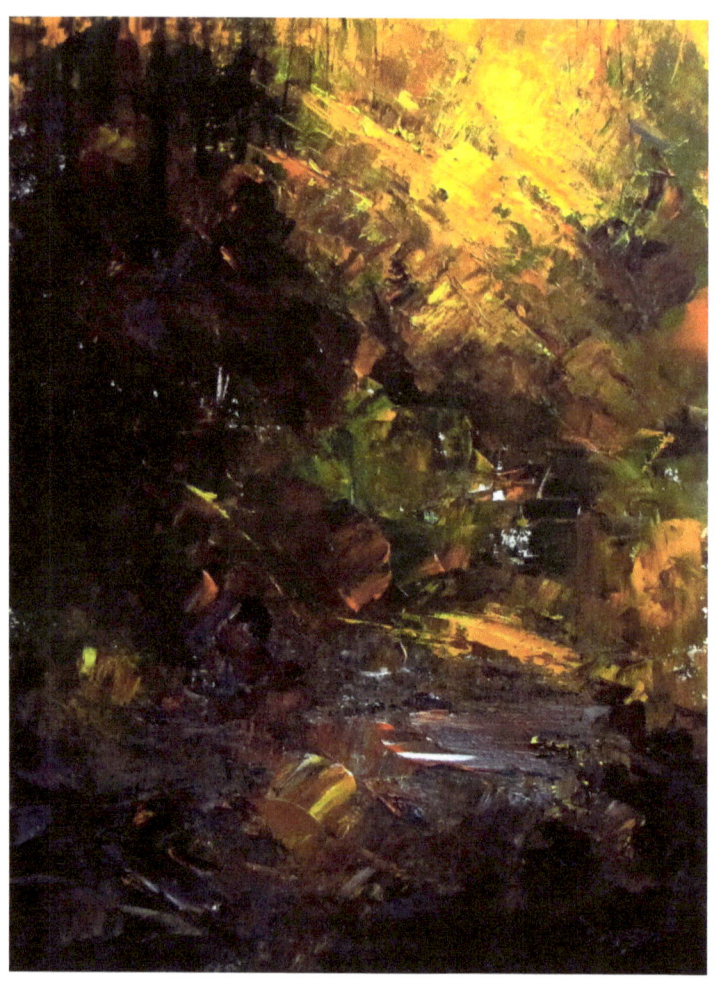

I felt painting is in its last stage. I checked for the corrections needed. I decided to add a few trees beside the centre of interest. It will serve two purposes, first, it will make the viewer to look at centre of interest area for a few more moments, second it will create spatial depth. Coming to this conclusion, I added trees. Usually with this painting will be over.
But … Sometimes game will continue.
Yes. To me it's not doing a painting. It's a game. Win or lose I will enjoy it.

Imagination plays a key role

Once the painting is finished, then everything is over. After that all you have to do, is sign it and keep it for sale. In that situation, where is the space for further imagination? What's the point of it?
Here is the fun.
For imagination, there is no end. It's infinite. You can go to any extent. That is what I do with every one of my paintings.
Here also it happened.

Few hours after, again I came back to the painting to look at it one more time, to convince myself what I have done is good.
I sat in front of it and started to observe it.
Few moments passed.
Then I felt it's better to continue it some more to make some changes. Dear student, I am warning you … sometimes these changes would spoil the painting which is already finished and good. But don't bother about it. If you want to play fully with your imagination you have to take that risk, whether you win or lose. Otherwise there is no sense in doing it. I always do that way. That's why whenever I do painting I will enjoy it irrespective of end results.
So I moved forward to make some changes in this painting.

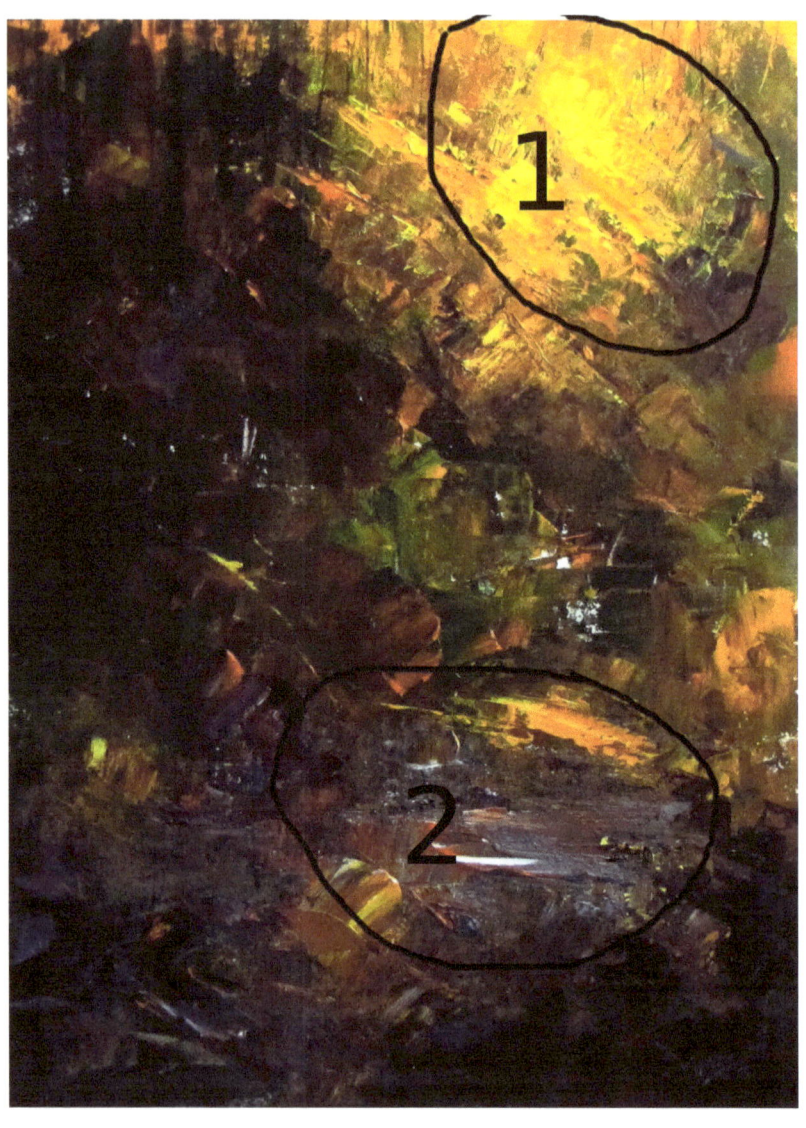

I would like to do same changes in the places marked 1 and 2. 1 is the centre of interest area. I felt it needed some more depth which will take the viewer more towards the inside of the forest mass. That depth will create mystery which I like.
And 2 … Here I want some blue violet color to balance the

yellows, yellow oranges and yellow greens in the painting. To put blue violet again I have to create water there which will occupy significant space.

Here is the fun.

You may ask me... ' previously, you said that water pond will make the eye movement pause for a bit before it moves to the centre of interest area. So to avoid that you said you were replacing the streak of water in the space of pond. Now again you want to paint water there in a considerable space. Now, is it not going to obstruct the eye movement? '

My answer is …; Yes, that was true in previous conditions. But situations changed now. One is centre of interest has more depth now, second I am not going to paint pond which has definite boundaries which will attract the eye movement for long. Instead of that, what I am going to paint is a feeling of moving water with blue violet color. So there won't be any problem for eye movement from bottom to top. (See the next picture)

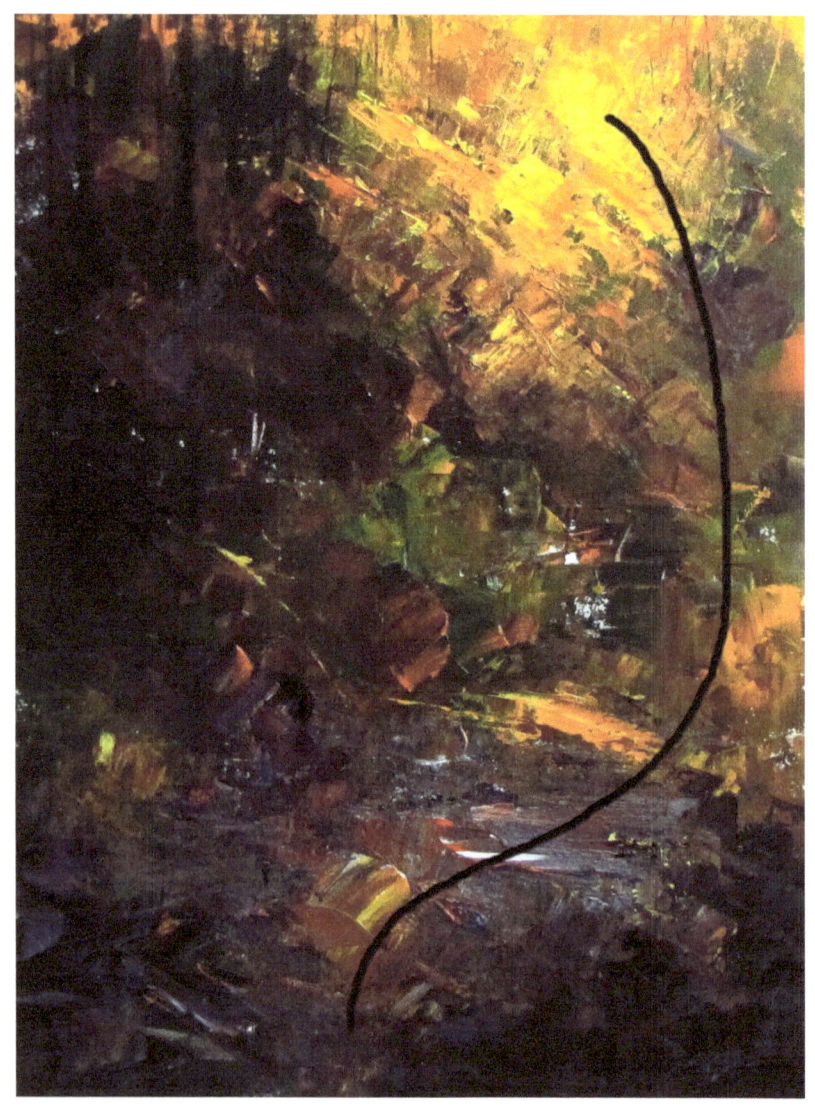

Final Painting

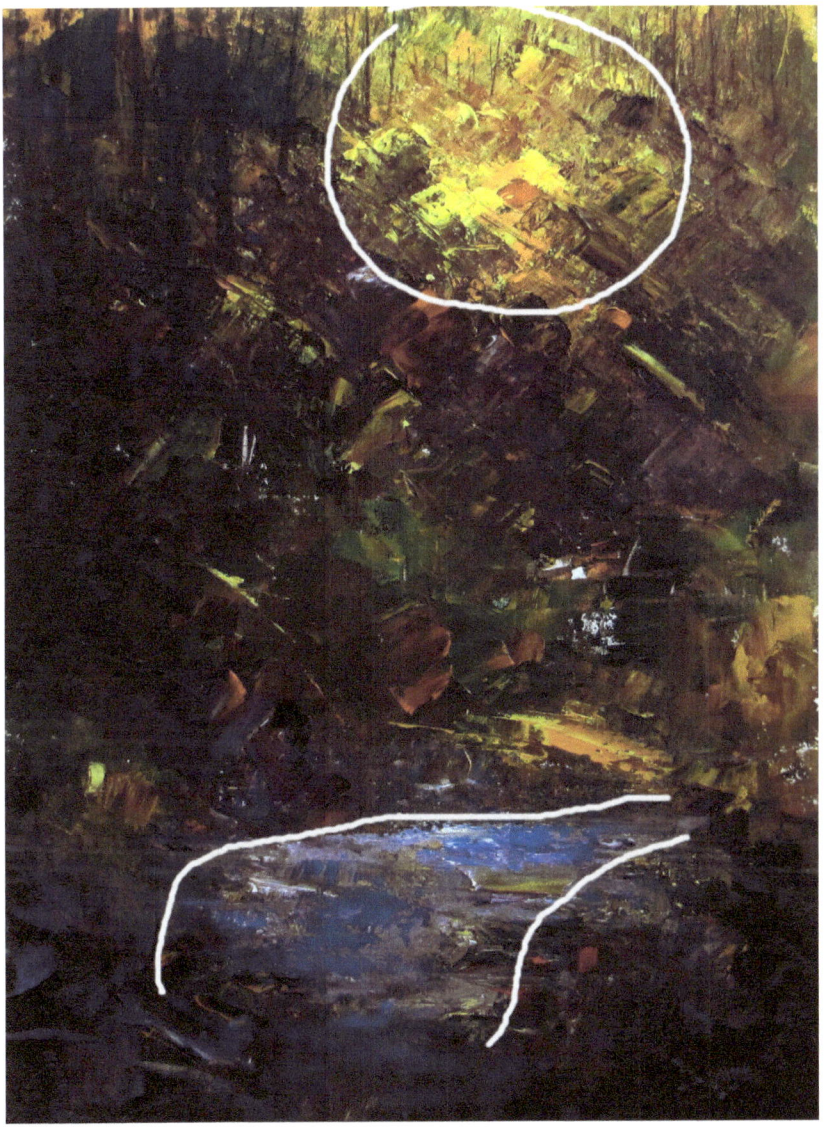

Observe the changes what I have done at the top and bottom

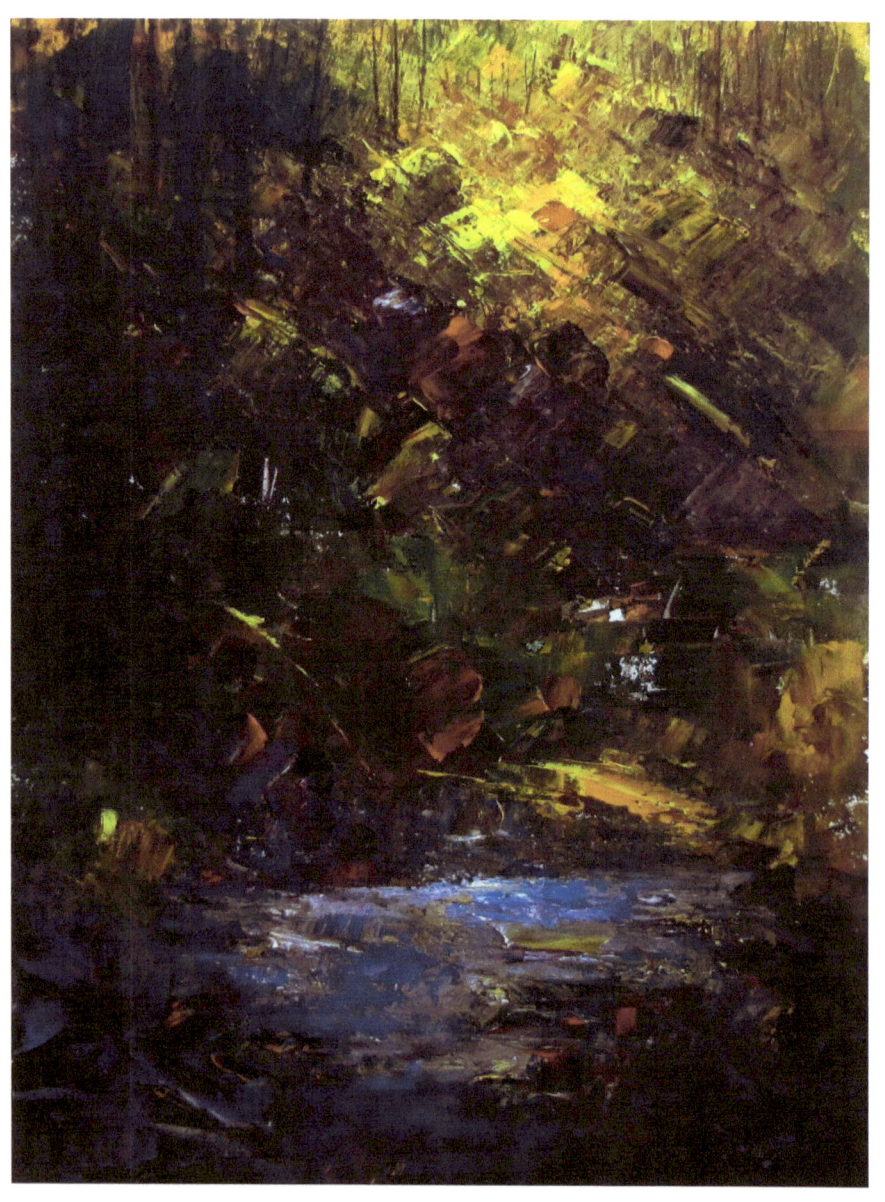

Page is Intentionally Blank

After 2 days

After two days I decided to work some more on this painting to satisfy myself. So I worked on it. This is the result. (On the next page)

My final words ... Everything in this universe has its own limits whereas your imagination does not have any.

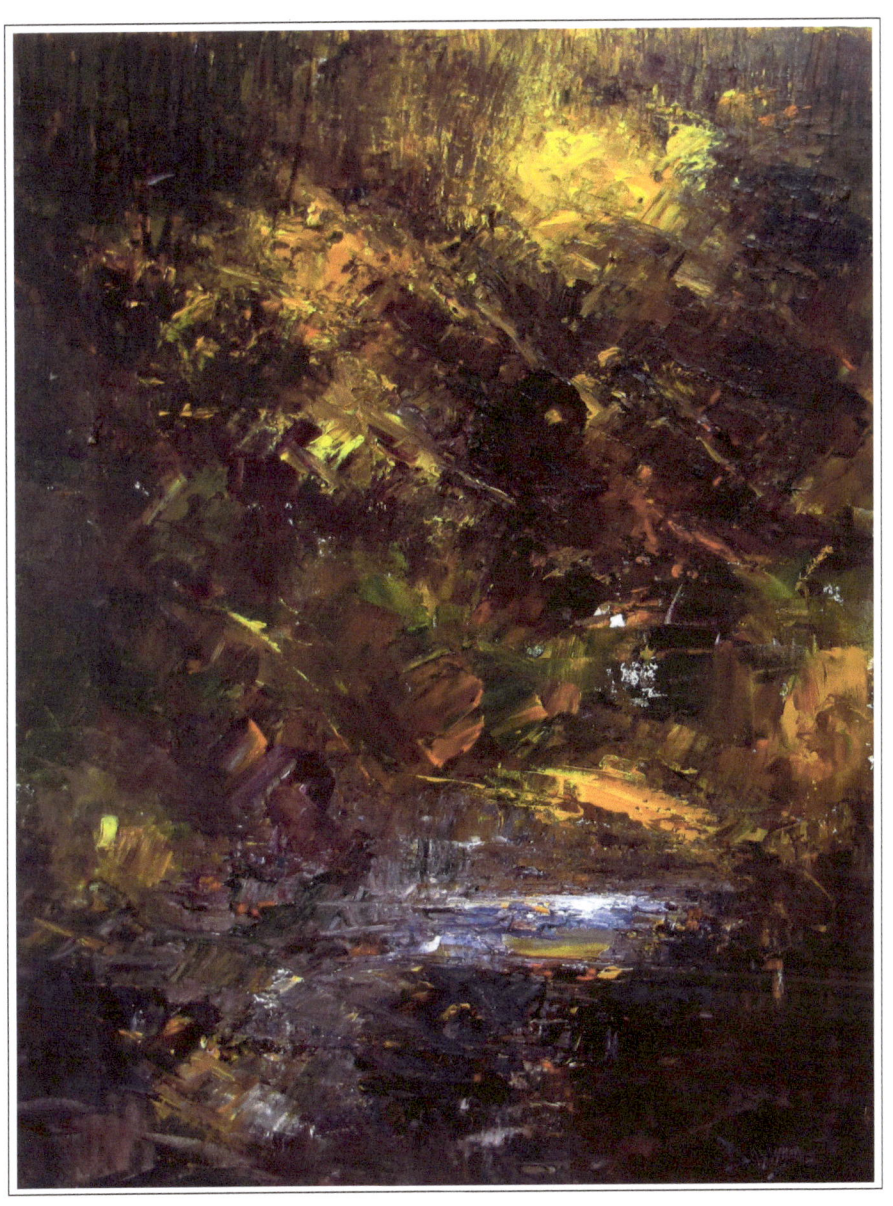

Concluding Words ...

Since few years I have been doing landscapes from imagination in both monochrome and color. That act of painting itself is an exciting factor for me to continue as an artist. When I was writing about that experience, I enjoyed a lot. This experience is inspiring me to write a few more books on this subject. I hope it will happen.

-Magunta Dayakar
 Hyderabad, India.

About Magunta Dayakar

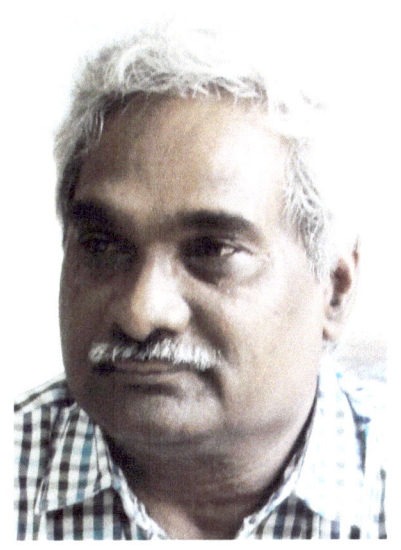

Magunta Dayakar was born in 1951 in Andhra Pradesh, India. After discontinuing his studies in graduation, he did different things in different periods. He had become a popular fiction writer in his native language Telugu, credited with thirty five novels. He had worked as an editor and also published a feature magazine for a brief period. He scripted, acted and directed two feature films. He ran Creative Painting School for children in Hyderabad for nearly 15 years.

He believes artist must be able to do all kind of subjects from Still life to Portraits, different styles like Abstract to Realistic Painting rather than limiting themselves to one or two subjects and styles, he strongly feels that is the only way any artist will be alive in his journey to understand the Science of Painting.

Now, most of the time he is working on writing books on painting. He defines science of painting as …"Just like there are Elements in Nature, there are a few elements in Art also. These elements can be played with using principles(tools) of Composition. Whatever art form you may work with, this knowledge is a must. If not, your work looks like a work of craft rather than a work of art."

Dayakar lives in Hyderabad and is spending all his time with Reading, Writing and doing Paintings. He is not interested in mixing with people, likes only to live with his work other than his family and a few friends.
He says…" Even thousand years is not enough to master the art, so it is meaningless to waste my time with other things. I am not having that luxury. I am destined to understand Art."
He strongly believes what he says and has been living that way.
He lives in Hyderabad, India

Website: https://maguntadayakar.com

My Books on Art (Available on Amazon)
How to Start a Painting and How to Plan it?
How to Finish a Painting?
Learn Composition and Create Beautiful Paintings

www.ingramcontent.com/pod-product-compliance
Lightning Source LLC
Chambersburg PA
CBHW040235220526
45473CB00001B/255